ACCOLADES

by

FARRUKH AHMAD

Translated from the
Bangla 'Sirajam Munira'

by

YASMIN FARUQUE

ISBN: 978-1-4669-8812-5 (sc)
ISBN: 978-1-4669-8811-8 (e)

Trafford rev. 04/17/2013

 www.trafford.com

North America & international
toll-free: 1 888 232 4444 (USA & Canada)
phone: 250 383 6864 ✦ fax: 812 355 4082

CONTENTS

DEDICATION vii

ACKNOWLEDGEMENTS ix

BIOGRAPHY OF THE POET xi

BIOGRAPHY OF THE TRANSLATOR xvii

PREFACE xix

SIRAJAM MUNIRA MUHAMMAD MUSTAFA...............................1

ABU BAKR SIDDIQ(R)..17

OMAR THE MAGNANIMOUS...22

OSMAN GHANI..32

ALI HAIDAR...38

FOLLOWER OF LOVE 47

GHAUSUL AZAM 48

KHWAJA NAKSHBAND..49

MUJADDID ALFESANI 50

MY MIND 51

PERIL OF DEATH..52

SULTAN OF HIND..53

TEARS DROP BY DROP..54

THE CASCADE 55

THE EXPLORER'S ENTREATY 56

THE INKLING 57

THE MARTYRS OF KARBALA 62

THIS STRUGGLE TODAY 66

THIS TUSSLE 70

DEDICATION

To my father, Dr. R. A. Ghani
And mother, the late Mrs Hosne Ara Ghani
Whose love has been, is and always will be inspiring for me.

ACKNOWLEDGEMENTS

This book would be sadly incomplete if I do not acknowledge the assistance and encouragement I received from quite a few people. Thanks are due to Dr. Motiur Rahman, President, Farrukh Academy, Dhaka, for graciously permitting me to translate this beautiful book. I am thankful to my parents for their love and encouragement. To my husband, Dr. Saleh Faruque, thanks are due for bequeathing the lion's share of his free time to the best presentation my little book could hope for. To my darling son, Shams, I say thanks for being my most ardent supporter.

BIOGRAPHY OF THE POET

Farrukh Ahmad was born in the village of Majh Ail, in Sreepur of Magura district, Bangladesh, on June 10, 1918. His father was Khan Sahib Syed Hatem Ali, and mother, Roushan Akhtar. In 1924, when Farrukh was only five years old, his mother died.

His schooling began in his small village open-air school. Then he attended the Kolkata Model M.E. School and the Baliganj High School. He graduated, however, from the Khulna Zilla School, passing in the First Division, in 1937. At high school, he had as teachers such noted writers as the poet Ghulam Mustafa, writer Abul Fazal, and the poet Abul Hashim. At Baliganj he had among his classmates Abdul Mannan Syed, later a writer and journalist of note, and Satyajit Roy, later a popular writer and filmmaker.

In 1937, his first poem 'Ratri' appeared in the magazine 'Bulbul,' edited by Habibullah Bahar (August). Another poem 'Pap Janma' came out in the periodical 'Muhammadi' edited by Mohammad Akram Khan, the same month. His first short story, 'Antarleen,' came out in the 'Muhammadi', too. He wrote the stories 'Biborno,' 'Mrito Basudha,' 'Ze Putul Dollyr Ma,' 'Procchonno Nayika,' etc., which came out one by one during 1937-9. When his teacher Abul Fazal went to Kolkata, Farrukh requested a copy of Walt Whitman's classic <u>Leaves of Grass</u>. Literary liaisons among Farrukh and the poet Ahsan Habib, writer Abu Rushd etc. were formed. Farrukh enrolled at Ripon College, Kolkata, where he had celebrities such as Vishnu De, Buddhadev Basu, and Pramathanath Bishi etc. as teachers. At this time a bouquet of Farrukh's poetry was published in the magazine 'Kobita,' edited by Buddhadev Guha.

In 1938, an illustrated treatise entitled 'Mr. Jonab Ali to the Exercise Instructor' was published. Allama Sir Muhammad Iqbal, the philosopher-poet, passed away. Farrukh wrote a bouquet of poems entitled 'Smarani,' dedicated to the memory of Iqbal. Poem 'Andharer Swopno' came out in the monthly Saogat, published from Kolkata. Farrukh contributed regularly to this magazine until 1947.

In 1939, Farrukh passed his I.A. (Now H.S.C.) examinations, and got admitted to the Scottish Church College, Kolkata, in the Honors College of Philosophy, for the Bachelor's degree. Poets such as Suvash Mukherji and Fateh Lohani were classmates. World War II began.

In 1941, Farrukh quit Scottish Church College and got admitted to Kolkata City College with Honors in Bangla Literature. Rabindranath Tagore, the Universal Poet, passed away in August. Poetic Bangla translations of some Koranic verses were published entitled 'Kabye Koran.' The poet transformed some of his ideals in the light of the Lahore resolution of 1940.

In 1942, the poet tied the knot with his cousin Tayyeba Khatun. He wrote a poem entitled 'Upahar' on the occasion of his marriage; the poem was published in the 'Saogat.' Kazi Nazrul Islam, the Poet of National Awakening (Now Poet Laureate of Bangladesh) falls ill of an incurable disease.

In 1943, Farrukh joined the office of the IG Prisons. He recited the poems 'Dal Bandha Bulbuli' and 'Biday' at the seventh session of

Bongiyo Mussalman Sahitya Sangsad. The poet began writing poems for Sat Sagorer Majhi, Sirajam Munira and Kafela. He also wrote poems on the drought of 1942-3.

Sat Sagorer Majhi, the poet's first volume of poems, was published in 1944. A poem entitled 'Lash' came out in the periodical 'Akal,' edited by the young poet Sukanto Bhattacharyya. Farrukh quit his job at the office of the IG Prisons to join the Kolkata Civil Supplies Office. His father, Syed Hatem Ali, died on Nov. 10.

Kazi Abdul Wadud, the spokesman for the Liberation of Intellect Movement, was hopeful about Farrukh's poetry in a speech at the Writers' Conference of PEN in 1945. Poems 'Shikar', 'Hey Nishanbahi' and 'Sat Sagorer Majhi' were published in the poetry journal 'Malancha', edited by Abdul Kadir and Rezaul Karim. The editorial emphasized Farrukh's poetry. The poet joined the staff of the periodical 'Muhammadi.' An untoward incident led to his resignation about a year later.

The poetry chapbook Azad Karo Pakistan was published in 1946. The poet recited a poem entitled 'Nijer Rokto' on Kolkata Radio. It may be mentioned here that the poet would participate in the program 'Golpodadur Ashor' on Akashbani Radio. The poet worked briefly at a company in Jalpaiguri.

-In 1947 Farrukh was unemployed after quitting his job at the 'Muhammadi'. This year the essay 'Navin Kobi Farrukh Ahmad' by the poet Abdul Kadir was broadcast from Kolkata Radio. The poet left Kolkata for his in-laws' place Durgapur, in Jashore. Essay, 'Pakistan: Rashtrovasha O Sahityo' was published. Colonial rule ended. Independence of 1947 was achieved.

The poet and his family moved permanently to Dhaka in 1948. He joined Dhaka Radio as a casual artist. He began to write songs for radio. In addition to modern, patriotic, Gospel and songs praising the Prophet, the poet gave short talks, and wrote skits, musicals and lyrical dramas. During the 50s, Farrukh began to direct Kishore Majlish, an educational program geared towards teen-agers. The prose-play 'Raj Rajra' is published. The historic Language Movement begins.

In 1951 Farrukh shunned the program to celebrate the birth anniversary of Iqbal, in protest of not inviting young writers.

In 1952, the book Sirajam Munira was published. Farrukh was hired as a staff artist of the Dhaka Radio. Barkat, Salam, Jabbar, Rafiq, Shafiq, Shafiul and many others embrace martyrdom, inciting protests at Dhaka University and outside, starting at Dhaka Radio. Farrukh emerged vocal. He participated in the Islamic Cultural Conference, held in Dhaka.

In 1953, Farrukh Ahmad was sacked from Dhaka Radio, along with fifteen others. The ensuing 17-day strike by these artists played a significant part in re-instating them all, including Farrukh.

In 1957, Farrukh was a key participant in the centenary observance of the Independence Movement of 1857, composing poems and songs on the occasion.

In 1958, the verse-play Naufel O Hatem was broadcast on Dhaka Radio. The play was produced by Khan Ataur Rahman, who also played the starring role.

In 1960, Farrukh was awarded the Pride of Performance Award by the Pakistani President. He also received the Bangla Academy Award for Poetry, and was elected a Fellow of the Academy. In the Drama Week of Bangla Academy, the verse-play 'Naufel O Hatem' was performed.

In 1961 Farrukh's verse-play Naufel O Hatem came out in print. Farrukh went on an extensive Governmental tour of North and South Bangla. The poet was accorded a heartfelt reception at Dhaka

Hall, presided over by Prof. M. Abdul Hai. Syed Ali Ahsan, Prof. Munir Chowdhury, poet Ahsan Habib, Abul Hossain et. al. spoke on Farrukh's poetry. Poet Shamsur Rahman, Muhammad Muniruzzaman, Salma Chowdhury, Badrul Hasan, Shabnam Mushtari et. al. recited Farrukh's poems. A program of Farrukh's songs directed by singer Abdul Ahad was put on. Dr. Sirajul Islam Chowdhury read the reception letter to Farrukh here.

In 1963 Farrukh's poetry book Muhurter Kobita was published. His satirical poetry was published under a pen name in the 'Dholaikabyo' edited by Faruque Mahmud. The School of Bangla Language and Literature at the Dhaka University observed Bangla Language and Literature Week. On this occasion recitations of poetry starting with the Charyyapada and up to & including Farrukh Ahmad's poetry were organized. Prof. Rafiqul Islam recited Farrukh's poem 'Dahuk' here.

In 1965, 'Pakhir Basha,' a book of juvenile poetry, was published. Inspired by the Indo-Pakistani war, the poet composed such inspirational songs as 'Jangi Jawan Chalo Bir,' 'Shaheeder Khunoranga Kashmir,' 'Jehader Maidane Chalo Jai.'

Hatem Ta'yi came out in 1966. The poet was awarded the UNESCO Prize for his book Pakhir Basha and the Adamjee Award for Hatem Ta'yi. The poet went for the last time to Faridpur, to see his elder brother, Syed Siddique Ahmad. On his return he wrote the poems 'Boishakh,' 'Padma,' and 'Aricha Parghate,' among other well-known and celebrated poems. The poet spurned the Sitara I Imtiaz title conferred by the Pakistani president as a sign of patriotism.

In 1968, 'Harafer Chharda', a book of kids' poems, was published.

In 1969 came the juvenile poetry book Notun Lekha. 'Kobi Farrukh Ahmad,' a well-researched book by Sunitikumar Mukherji, was published. Noted artist Mustafa Aziz painted a portrait of the poet. Countrywide popular uprising of 1969 began.

In 1970 came the rhyme book <u>Chhardar Ashor</u>, Part I. The poet completed more than two decades with Dhaka Radio. This year the poet was featured on the editorial and cover of the fortnightly Elan (Now Radio Bangla), for the early November issue. National elections took place.

In 1971, the poet recited a poem on Dhaka Radio for the very last time. Bangladesh came into being after a bloody struggle.

1973 saw Farrukh facing a catastrophic dilemma at work after the liberation of Bangladesh. Essayist Ahmad Safa wrote an acerbic article, 'Farrukh Ahmader Ki Oporadh?' (What Crime Has Farrukh Ahmad Committed?) (Gonokontho, June 15). As a result, Farrukh was re-instated in the commercial activities of Radio Bangladesh, Dhaka.

The poet suffered physically and mentally for many everyday and social reasons. In June 1974 he wrote his very last poem: Famine 1974(A Pictograph). Apart from this he wrote poems in praise of God the Almighty and of the Prophet Muhammad (PBUH) and poems on Gaddafi, and translated a long Urdu poem on Maulana Shafiullah (Dadaji). Farrukh breathed his last on Oct. 19, at home in Eskaton Gardens, Dhaka.

In 1975, <u>Farrukh Ahmader Shreshtho Kobita</u> was published. Farrukh was honored with a posthumous Ekushey Padak for Literature in 1977, the posthumous Swadhinata Puroshkar in 1980, and the Islamic Foundation Award in 1984.

BIOGRAPHY OF
THE TRANSLATOR

Yasmin Faruque was born on Nov. 11, 1955, in Dhaka, Bangladesh. She attended Viqarun Nisa Noon Girls' High School, Holy Cross College and the School of English Literature at Dhaka University. She has written stories and poems since she was a mere child. The present work, Accolades, is her third attempt at translation. Her first, Moni Monjusha, a Bangla translation of short English poems, appeared in print in November 1979. Her second, Tribute to Tagore, a translation of Tagore's short stories, was published by Trafford in July 2012. Now married and the mother of an adult son, she lives in Grand Forks, ND, USA. Since 2005, she has presented stories, poems and essays at the Annual Writers' Conference at the University of North Dakota, Grand Forks. Eight of her book reviews were published in the Grand Forks Herald during 2005 and 2006.

PREFACE

Farrukh Ahmad(1918-74) is first and foremost a poet. He has been termed the poet of Muslim Renaissance. In reading his poems, we are struck by the blend of spiritualism and romanticism in them. This is his unique contribution. He stressed the ideal, though the real and the ideal find a harmonious co-existence in his works. His collection of poems <u>Sirajam Munira</u>, which I have translated as <u>Accolades</u>, bears testimony to this.

After Kazi Nazrul Islam, the Poet Laureate of Bangladesh, Farrukh is the first poet to call for a moral transformation for Muslims. He and Nazrul shared ideals and ideologies, though unlike Nazrul, Farrukh did move to Dhaka after partition in 1947. He worked at the then Radio Pakistan (Now Radio Bangladesh) for a number of years.

Farrukh's philosophy of life was shaped by Islamic ideology. That is not to say, however, that he was a demagogue or a fundamentalist. Far from it, he espoused freedom of speech and action. <u>Accolades</u> has inspiring poems in it that would infuse new life into the most lethargic of souls.

In this beautiful volume there are poems about the Holy Prophet(PBUH), the four Caliphs, and other spiritual-romantic subjects. I have translated these poems to the best of my ability. I know I may have made mistakes. If, in spite of those, my readers accept this book, I shall be amply rewarded.

Yasmin Faruque
Grand Forks ND 2013

SIRAJAM MUNIRA
MUHAMMAD MUSTAFA
(PEACE BE UPON HIM)

There he rises, above the Eastern horizon like an emperor

His sign flies constantly against the clear

blue sky, ever before the wind

O Bird of Light! Hast thou awakened?

Roaming the wide blue yonder

Will the night-silenced voice burst forth in a song of light?

Is a tearful note being strummed from the prison of peace?

What dream of light will make the turbulent waters

Turn from their course?

Say, will the deaf-mute sky now forget its silence

When the long-distance traveler calls in his affectionate, ringing

Yet silent tones?

Lo, here flits that bird on its searing white

Yet resplendent rainbow wings

As the sky intensifies its deep turquoise clarity

The dog-footed night is pained

And vanishes in a mere moment

In the golden radiance

While the static lightning dances in time

To tunes made of light waves.

O Bird unknown! From what depth of sky

hast thou soared yonder?

The beat of thine wings has made

The blossom of language and expression bloom forth.

1

With thy ribbon of golden thread
thou measurest the mindset of the world
As golden islands emerge suddenly on unfamiliar oceans.

All the oceans' tears sparkle on thine eloquent wings
The scarlet lotus of youthful thought kisses thy shadow.
O winged messenger of radiance! Thou knowest
All the rays of the unfettered blue out that window
The inkling of that velocity has thus given rise
To the universal dream.
Thou art not of the darkest of blind nights, nor art thou
Of death's stillness.
Thou hast flung open all the doors of the heavens and the mind
The welkin is a-quiver with emotion, looking out
At the path thou wilt come by.
O open-winged light! Thou hast blest the earth
By thine arrival.
'Who is it that cometh?' rises the tumult
'Who cometh, who cometh?' the new to-do also gathers speed
As the deep-slumbering, nay dead, locality wakes up after a century.
To rekindle our senses in us, thou bringest the precious Water of Life.
I know, O dear Sirajam Munira, thine rays awaken myriads of morns
In thine lightning-sparks are hidden a thousand days and nights
And in those rays awaken Siddique, Zinnurain and a youthful Ali
And Lo! Here is Al Faruque too, awakened
out of the profoundest of slumbers,
Observing that bright morning light.
In thine liberal, unhindered radiance are numerous tongues of flame
Pulsing with life-giving light.

If thou wert not here, the nectar-urn of the

world would never have been looted

And drained dry

If thou camest not, the narcissus would not have opened her calyx

The lover's heart, agog with peculiar desires

Would not have flung open its innermost core.

The sun, sentinel of daylight, would never have removed

The drapes of waning darkness.

Thus when this Prophet of Prophets came down to this Earth

The world watched in open-mouthed astonishment his comely form

Aglow in celestial grace.

In his right hand was a thunderbolt, in his left a blooming rose.

His heart, dusky with dust, held the whole world.

When the passengers of the sullied eventide

beheld before them the lion's range.

Just at that moment, O Illustrious One,

thou brought'st the lighted lamp

O Shepherd, Prophet of the World! From

you we learned who indeed we are

Your picture shines forth in the brightness of the Sun of Time

Here came he, who walked like a pauper, yet regally too

The flower of his tender heart bruised by the thorn

Even yet, he diffused the aroma of musk. In the sandy desert

Bloomed fresh pomegranate blossoms

Just as the touch of Abraham made the resentful fire

Bloom out, like so many flowers.

I have observed thine humanity move

With the great body of the general public

Who beautified this their earthly abode with such flowers

As they found blooming along muddy paths.

Even there, yet even there, thou hast made crops grow
And copious showers fall
Even then, O even then, have the blind ones awakened?
Oblivion has concealed thy days from these modern times.
Does this faded image of ugliness invade the beauty therein
Keening the hunger that coils like a python and
bursts forth hot like tongues of fire
Hurting in poignant pain. I beheld the Heavens
Unconscious under his venomous breath. The Bird of Light, O Sun,
Forgets the song of the road
Thou hast taught it.
I remember that potent venom, a cloud on the Arab horizon.
O what suffering and anxiety for the victims of the tormentors!
The purchased slaves are beaten to pulp like mute beasts
As if the season for killing babies has arrived at last
Making land and water quake under that heavy burthen of sin.
People devoid of personality and humanity, drunk on blood and wine
Crowd the city sewers
Smearing fecal matter on an unsullied forehead
like animals devoid of taste or decency
Whose eyes are bleared with adultery,
pluralism and hedonistic identities
They put idols in the Holy Ka'aba, bowing blindly to them
While crowds of destitute orphans roam the
streets, groaning in unspeakable agony
And wipe their teary eyes, though it be useless
Because their oppressors beat them.
Even today I seem to hear them choking
newborn girl-babies to death,

The dying screams of those helpless ones
making the date-palm leaves tremble
In silent empathy.
Burying those corpses in the desert sands gladdens those hard hearts,
While Mother Earth weeps, clutching her lifeless babes to her breast.
The purchased slaves, humans all, fell at the hands of specters,
Who skinned them as butchers do.
True religion had then been all but effaced from the face of the earth
And the Earth, her face downcast in shame,
descended into infamy at a frightening pace.
Thou, O Sunshine of the entire world, came
down with a ray of light in thy heart.
Did the earth quake that day
As Nausheroan's portals broke wide open, and
The magic inferno lit by a millennium of idol-worship went flat out?

Does the little lambkin throw out her mouthful of sweet grass
To listen to an unfamiliar tune,
And the rays of the setting moon crave the tide
In broad daylight?
Oh, the destitute, fatherless orphan who just
Swings in play on his mother's lap!
And one day he loses his mother too
Drying his tears the poor child roams the streets alone.
The little one herding sheep in the fields has
felt profoundly this piercing pain
Traversing the trade-routes with the burden made
him realize the tribulations of humanity.
In the hot winds and intense sunshine the
desert pebbles scatter and fly

As the fiery rays smite your comely form with white-hot arrows.
From the northwest comes a tempest of desert sands
The adolescent throat parches in thirst, the
stomach aches in the throes of hunger
As all his nerves seem on the verge of a
breakdown in the direst want imaginable.
Acacia thorns scratch his body, his back
gives way to the heavy burthen,
His tears fall fast as his heart's blood spills on the Syrian sands.
O dear youth, you spend your nights on hard pillows of date-leaves.
I know not what unflinching artisan smites the
stone again and yet again with hard knocks
Looking repeatedly at it, making sure it's to his liking.
Searing a thousand days in the desert furnace of a myriad sufferings
He tints your most beauteous heart in the hues of pain.
Then your large heart has understood the tribulations of the destitute
Being hungry itself has made it realize the pain of the famished
And the sadness of the captive sons of Adam; where yet
The pain of the woman is.
What artisan has brought tears to those huge eyes of yours?
Searing a thousand days in the desert furnace of a myriad sufferings
He tints your most beauteous heart in the hues of pain.
O, what artisan has brought tears to those huge eyes of yours?
The very depth of the desert welkin pales
before that magnanimous heart
You dole out your portion of dates without taking any yourself.
Then there came those days of meditation in the dark Cave of Hera,
Where thou sit'st in the dark, meditating,
O, in that tide floats the ark seeking the
ultimate truth, alone and friendless

Al Amin, lit by the light of truth, apple of the desert Makkah's eyes
Searches for the root realization, the love-lit, ultimate reality,
The searing desert breath makes the sands change place
The portal of the day closes, as the dark door of night opens
In the deep azure glow a myriad of sleepless stars
Thou, O Meditator, pass thine night in sad sleeplessness, too.
Your sky and your mind are still and unmoving
You seek salvation for the soul with the
desert thirst parching your throat.
Restless in the very hope, thou seek'st the elixir
of life on the summit of the Hera
And at the end of the sun-weary day descends
your long night of meditation.
Lighting up all the stars of eagerness like so many lamps
You, O Silent Meditator, seek the One and Only Truth
The Creator Al Ahad.
You seek in the Oneness the great Truth of Knowledge.
What seek you with those thirsting eyne as
they fill with tears of utter dejection?
O Intense Concentrator, thou who art alone and destitute
What olive-flavored memory keeps thee untiringly awake
The whole night through?
Does the desert sun not burn thee, nor the stones of Hera
Pierce the soles of thy feet?
What quest for enlightenment made thee leave thy peaceful abode
In the oasis ring of date palms?
O, does the parched, thirsting wind concede to that emotion?
The fire of passionate love makes the whole body quake
As trees in a storm.
The flood of tears that dims your eyes like the tears of the Al-Burj

Asks in a weepy voice when its wait-time,

the night of silence, will end.

The dew shines on the olive branches while the

world of Arab-Azam lies fast asleep

O Sleepless Ones! Before you wakes the morn

pale after the night wanes.

Even then thy stars twinkle undimmed through the longest of nights.

Those eyne toil tirelessly seeking the ultimate knowledge.

Lean and sere, the body breaks down, the

mind unhinged with weeping

At this time, Oh what a tornado did whirl

in, churning up the desert sands

And the hourglass of time tolled the great news down

Radiant in that Eternal Light the constant Truth

blazing forth bright as the noontide sun

Is held the Knowledgeable Koran, which came down

In your voice, O Lost Bird!

What dim glow-worm prest under the sylvan lightning

Lit the Eternal Light in your mind, all over everywhere.

Quoth it, 'Read'-he was the kindhearted Jibrail(A)

You, Oh Shepherd-Prophet, came up like a picture

And stood before that ocean of knowledge, O silent sun of the Hera!

The date-palms stood still, silhouetted against the sky at that moment

The astounded world watched wide-eyed the power

Of this, one of her illustrious sons.

The blue, star-spangled Heavens are throwing open their portals

O Prophet, as you read in the Name of your Lord.

As you stood on that dusty desert road

With the light of the Holy Koran illuming your heart

Watching sorrowfully the people, being drawn into

A whirlpool of sins.

Oh, the iniquities! Oh, the injustice! That horrible dusk engulfs all.

The century retches night and day on the path

Decking the Ka'aba out in dolls, they bow to these

So drunk are they in sin

As the illiterate cast their nets into the fog of ignorance

Throwing up the stale poison of dead indistinctness

That is dark and endless.

You planted the olive tree of enlightenment

On the dark pinnacle that day,

O Sirajam Munira, and came forth, like a light

That awakens a myriad of spirits.

You climb the impassably rocky summit,

With a desire to deliver mankind.

Blood flows from your wounds as you scale each stony wall

O Hero! There you step as firmly as a rock

Traversing the stony expanse, you salve the sick

With the touch of the fountain.

O Prophet Muhammad(PBUY)! The day you called forth the Truth

From the crest of the Safa'a

Myriads of rivers flowing blood came forth and

stood before you. 'There is no God but Allah,

And Muhammad(PBUH) is His Prophet'

The day you declaimed this, the whirlpool

Of darkness and errors burst with a thunderclap.

The light-blinded carnivores came that day with all they'd got

To devour. You, O unmoved Messenger of Allah,

Stood stalwart as a rock.

These stony hearts, rusted as they are with abuse,

Desire the scratching out of these petals of light in thorns.

The stones resist, Abu Jihil, the Devil personified, wakes up.

On these hills you spend your long days of interment

Even the food of animals does not dim your smile so bright

Bathed in blood at Ta'ayef you declaim 'He is

The One and Only, without partners,'

O Sun of the Hera! Even as the sky remains hidden

under a curtain of all-engulfing darkness

When the blow to your blood makes your body and mind fall apart

Even then you meditate, seeking out the Light of Truth

Even then, O even then the shroud of knowledge is drawn apart,

And the search goes on, untiring.

O Wayfarer of Knowledge! The Ocean whose tides make

Night and Day come forth

O Two-Toned Bird! You spread your wings

Over those endless waters

And dive under to seek out the pearls of untold wisdom.

When you asked, 'Who is Muhammad?' Ayesha replied not.

Who on this earth has the depth of knowledge

To realize who Muhammad really happens to be?

You yourself are aware of your nonentity,

the chronicle of the earth, and

The legacy of the Lord Almighty, Master of Mankind

That makes the idea fly up to the sky in sparks of light.

The soil has received in its loving arms the tornado

That makes the Heavens quiver

And that the ferociously lit desert Simoom can traverse

In a mere instant

The stars of the nebulae scatter from the embrace

of the bewitching twilight

And the whole Heavens surrender to his huge strong grasp.

And then his quiet sky expands in the worshipful evening
When the Earth weeps, recollecting her own poignant tale of woe.
On such a still, dark night Borraq bore the Radiance down
Starry night, sunny morning and a lightning-swift storm.
I know not how many heavens you crossed
Before you donned the crown of pearls for the very first time.
That first night of waiting was also the first full night
Of the celestial journey.
That night the earth's populace knew the full extent of your legacy
That even now makes the pomegranate flowers bloom.
Even yet the desert mentality of Makkah did
not accept your life-giving waters
The Oasis of Madinah, however, did extend to you
Her hand in welcome.
Even there the hostile Makkans did not leave you alone
But stabbed you with their venomous knife of hatred
And surrounded you with death and destruction at Badar and Ohud
Even then as Commander-in-chief you kept your cool
A million forms of death stalked you, yet, O great soldier,
Afraid you were not
The luster of that body made Ali Haidar stare in amazement
The stalwart Hamza thrilled in pleasure that his weapon
Had come awake
Taking in hand the two-edged sword he shouted,
'Hail, Soldier! Victory to ye.'
One hand-signal from ye, and the desert fort is unlocked
By the sun-baked, famished throngs in procession
Then came the Day of Victory your Lord had promised
In full glory came Fathum Mubin—a day lit up
In the radiance of peace

Roses bloomed in profusion as Bil'al called for prayers

In the wait of a protracted night among the desert thorns.

Unfaltering is your patience, O Prophet! It is

A wonderful thing, all-beautiful

And in your eyes awaken the myriads of ancient, distant coffers.

From those re-awakened troves the Sindbad of those

Seven seas, unseeing, pond-like

Tears the salt waters asunder to bring to port a new day

And cuts through the blue ocean-waves to raise the Marjan crop

Where the far-going celestial navigator spreads his wings

To cultivate on the sun's rays the valley denuded by night

Where the sorrowing lovebird finds his mate again

Along a forgotten pathway.

From the horizon the full moon bears forth a load of fragrance

And the juicy pomegranate bursts in the gardens of Jerusalem.

Where, O where indeed did the dirt of wrongdoing,

Slime and adultery conceal itself?

And where is the venom of the inhuman passenger's heart?

His chains have shattered, Paradise lies underfoot.

Holding a vivacious, vibrant baby the mother weeps

Tears of sheer joy.

Horde upon horde of new horn-blowers emerge,

These masses that are infused with a new zest for life

The whole fortune fills with a pious word the endless blue,

Land and sea

And even the irreligious debater acknowledges

The Oneness of Allah Almighty

"Allah is our Lord, and Muhammad(Pbuh) is

His Prophet, I know for certain

The Son of the Desert, with his companion the great Suffa

Has comprehended the truth. Life-giving waters

Have made centuries-old corpses come awake once again.

The Eternal knowledge has set the dead, broken lamp-holder alight

The Heavens resound with that clarion call, with the leaves

Echoing that call for prayers

Have you raised that colorful brush to the stormy sky by mistake?

Lo! You stopped that fierce storm only in the wink of an eye.

The inkling of a journey awoke in the jagged white road-line

And released the seven-layered sweet waters

That had lain dormant for so long

The dry sands have become wet, hearts fill with tears of love

The lover and the nightingale both crave

Those dew-drenched pink petals.

So there breaks a wave of happiness in the heart

Of Wayes Karani, the humble farmer who loved not big crowds.

Only you know how indeed he passes his days.

You emptied a coffer of wealth, O Great One!

Yet in that rude mud hut the tears of sympathy were for eternity.

You wielded the cobbler's needle yourself; like a porter

You carried loads of bricks.

O, did you indeed fill that torn bag of yours with beatings

From the Jews?

What wealth of gifts is in your heart for your disciples,

And indeed for all mankind,

And how meekly you do submit to the Supreme Lord.

The old moon wanes, yielding place to the new

And again that moon has burst forth, black as coal

After crossing the blue desert sands

How many pieces of broken moon crowd around your doorstep

Even then, O King of Makkah and Madina,

Your home faces dire want

There's not a scrap of food cooking on the stove,

You spend so many nights empty

Even then, for your disciples, indeed for all mankind,

You shed many tears.

No lamp dispels the gloom in your hut, the flame burning instead

In your compassionate heart

In that clay lamplighter glows the dream

Of a red Firdaus.

The volcanoes have erupted, setting the skies aflame,

And the people have awakened with you.

Your followers have not let even dire failure dampen their resolve.

Thus has Siddiq attained the Sea of Truth in his heart

And thus is there such a clamor of the world's populace

In Omar's hut, formed of leaves and branches—

And just so did the door to Osman's incomparable spirit fly open

Yes, just thus did the curved lightning of Ali's Zulfiqar

Flash out in his hands.

The lover's heart-strings are taut with desire

As Khalid and Tariq unfurl the flag.

Turning their caravans towards the great China

Seekers of knowledge hie themselves thither.

With sails up, the sailboats ply the river

Between ebb and flood tides

As myriads of rivers fill and flow with new waters

And as these too seek new destinations to quench their thirst

Making seasonal flowers bloom out along their banks

And collecting year-end harvests.

Bequeathing all your expenses to your people,

O Sun of the Desert, art thou unmindful now?

Has the time come at last for a fresh journey
Along a pathway seldom traveled?
Has the Darling called? Did the Great Artisan
Call from high up in the Seven Heavens?
O Prophet, having filled the desert sky with light
Where now will the sun be needed?
Is this your evening arbor? Where have your jasmines bloomed?
What radiant magnolia dell has made this soil iridescent?
In what rose-garden of heaven has the Si bird begun to warble?
You departed leaving the earth and flowers of that soil in the sands
Where the fragrant petals of the rose flash deep pink
With the eternal elixir.
You, O Moon of Liberation, hied yourself there in its shadow.
Every grain of sand on your path still beckons an invitation.
The forest is immersed in a dream, splashing the soil
In droplets of green.
Your index finger still points to the Heavens,
And lo & behold! You still weep
For your injured disciples all over the world.
Your gravesite is still fragrant with that heavenly scent.
The odor of the camellia and the floods of tears are still there.
The hero of Jilan, the Chishti hero comes forth
With the flame of knowledge and meditation
In making his spirits thrill Nakshband weeps copious tears
The Mujaddid of millennia have unfurled the pennant
Of knowledge and love
The militant Dileer of Roybareilly has woken up
Out of the slumber of a million nights
They've borne your standard, leaving their mark
Yet their journey ended not, never ever to be finished

O Night, remembering your rays a myriad
Of lamp-holders burn bright
And a keen thirst for life makes this night raise her face.
Under the ash-gray skies there lurk tearful rains
Looking for new stars the nebula has lost its sight.
The expansive background hesitates over you
Like a raging desert storm over the alluvium
Of limitless possibilities.
To those who imprint their bold footprints on this new soil,
Cutting through the crisp yet senseless dark of paralysis
I bid peace, and to you too, O King of Men
O Prophet! To you, peace! Peace be upon you
Always, O Messenger of Allah!

ABU BAKR SIDDIQ(R)

When after a night spent in the desert
Orion the Brave came down
The date-palms of faraway Madinah
Lost their veil of profound darkness.
Farewell, O welkin of Makkah!
The ancient date-palms will stay here still.
On the curved horizon has been drawn
The path that the caravan trod.
Even then, farewell, my dear olive-branches!
The whole atmosphere sings goodbye today
As with a broken sitar.
We twain have to travel the whole way
With only God Almighty as our guide
The date-leaves that blow down in this season's storms
Will soon grow out again as new ones.
Many days will pass without companions
Yet we three will never be alone.
The moon and stars have joined us as companions
Just a little bit too late.
In much disaster and inclement weather
The great Ark of Islam floats by itself
Even when serpent-infested impediments threaten to blot out
Its final pathway.
The sum of so many days' closed-off walls has raised
A pathetic moan
And myriads of minds have sunk deep into the oblivion
Of a dark night.

The desert soil is as dry as sand! We shall have
To traverse it by ourselves
The date-palms of Madina swish and sway in clear daylight
Although it seems night has descended here.

*   *   *   *

Then swing that Madina from sky to sky
Unfurl the white flag of peace over the date-palms
The vast old dignified ocean of profound peace
O thou ever-faithful, all-denying companion of the night of pain
O Friend Sublime! Unfurl the Pennant of Peace
Over the skies of Madinah,
A place that makes even a great hearted volcano like Omar quake.
O Magnanimous Soul! Thou stand'st there
Tearing the welkin asunder with an immovable truth
The waves of the expansive Atlantic blend
With those of the Pacific
And seek a haven of peace under a storm-tossed sky.

*   *   *   *

Your heart is large and tranquilly peaceful is your lap
The desert traveler plants there with a terrific clang
The flag that the Prophet(Pbuh) left on this earth as his final legacy.
O Great One! Epitome of Might! It spread its wings
From your hands.
O Caliph who left everything behind! We watched enthralled
As crowds thronged your doorstep
On the path of the desert-hard life these millions accompanied you.

All the wide-open doors of the Jannatul Firdaus call out to you
Hie thee hither, Siddiq! O Loving Companion who made friends
With the destitute
Giving away all wealth to the world.
The Moon of Peace has set towards the path to Firdaus.
Even to this day I see the tears of compassion and fellow-feeling
That the constant companion of the Prophet(Pbuh)shed
Ever and anon.
Even just so, no one can hinder his quest for the truth
And his bravado, that strikes down falsehood and dishonesty
Like a thunderbolt, is not to be conquered.

*   *   *   *

With your knees in the dust, you bow down on the sands
Bringing an image of the sweetest submission to mind.
You do not worship any other than Allah, Beneficent and Merciful
Nor own servitude.
As such, that great soul of yours rises, kissing only
The Throne of Allah Almighty
Thus, only thus can you radiate the unsullied silver rays
Of the moon
And bear the heavy burthen of the earth,
Moving it by a hand signal alone.
In the worn-out moonshine are the healthy young moonbeams
And in the dry soil the rosebush pokes out amusedly
Growing up in apparent negligence
In the brimful cauldron of life-forces
Into your alluvium the Dunes of Firdaus are mixt anon.

The moon, that had frozen into solid ice,

Melts at your warm touch.

Somewhere, a nightingale bursts forth her melodious notes;

The fiddle sings from the depths of the lover's heart.

You've crost over so many tempests, and yes,

Mile upon mile of desert sands as well.

And so, calm as a lake,

The sea stretches out before you.

The sere field that baked alone in the sun for so long

Is now green with so many date-palm fronds.

O Seeker of the Truth! Your busy life is now

As quiet as the calmest of skies.

The lightning, flashing out briefly from time to time

Only serves to heighten the sense of the profound bottomlessness.

O Meditating Mendicant of Ma'arefat! I know not

Where you step as you walk forth. I cannot understand.

Has the Ever-familiar yet always Unknown not been found

In all this seeking?

Standing at the doorstep of complete knowledge

Yet ignorant of it, you stay awake in profound silence.

When it is time, you respond with words

In the heart of the starlit sky.

O Lover! Yet you keep moving calmly

In the long day's journey into night.

In the collected meditation of all true believers

Shines your unsullied radiance.

In your untamed fragrance rises a tempest of wild henna;

Intoxicated by that aroma, the drunkard seeks again

That marble scent.

In some faraway places, as the evening iris drops,
The froth of that perfume drips in the breeze
That rose petal incense wafts in the desert wind
The intoxicating spice of Ambary Tobacco floats in from afar
Subtly scented like the sweetest of dreams.
In the heart the pure dire light gathers anon.
In utter amazement the maddened musk-deer
On the run, has fallen flat before that raging storm.
O Ascetic! Your mind is a pure land, a fragrant arbor
Of fresh blooms
Where the nightingale forgets to trill her melodious notes
As she meditates on that profound silence.
In the heart of the poignant, Absolute truth
Rises the voice of the distant wayfarer
And wafts upward the voice of the still unmoving desert
On a night twinkling with myriads of stars
'God is Great! Great is He indeed!'
Passing the night in the desert, you've been through many such,
O Orion, Brave One!
What you haven't laid eyes on, though, are the radiant
Nights of Meditations, by a sympathetic ally
Although it is dark here, the skies of Madinah are aglow
With morning sunlight,
And penetrating the veil of darkness here
The Earth's surface has lit up.

OMAR THE MAGNANIMOUS

I have seen him on the move . . . . the desert wayfarer
Where to, no one has any idea
With a heavy burthen on his back, traveling across
The sere, dead landscape, I know not by what attraction.
There he goes, carrying humanity across the lifeless desert
Pouring out his fiery life-force along the fields of Jerusalem.
Traversing the rocky road, the leader of the herd
Of camels goes onward.
Where even among the ways no feet have ever trod
People have set up home—
That is the road he has chosen to take.
All hills, walls of impediment—all bars
Such as these fly like dust before him.
There he goes, far afar, with just a servant for company.
The sun has lit up the sky with deadly fire
That heat burns the body as with searing flames
Yet joyously the camel-keeper pulls the tether-rope.
Satisfied with just a handful of dry dates
That representative of Muslims brought liberty
To all mankind, on the field of truth and justice.

*   *   *   *

O Omar! That day and this
Have been bound in an inexorable tie.

I know not when evening descended thence
The deep dark night has come down here
In that shadow.
Here there is only moaning
And no, not a word on you.
We lie prone like exhausted corpses
Because Omar is not here today.

*   *   *   *

But even so we know that the minds
Of the dust-begrimed masses don't stop
In the crooked Zulmat he seeks out
The Caliphate of Omar.
In that speed flares up his searching sunlight,
And before that momentum flies
A mountain of fear and apprehension.
O Omar! I wish I could see
Into that generous heart of yours.
However did you manage to bring
These tortured masses to the forefront,
O Great-hearted One, and travel onwards
With them?
How, and wherefore, did you color this sere desert
And bring forth a radiant white day?
O Caliph of the Oppressed! You chose the best path.
The Caliphate of your equality sits on this earthen throne.

Even to this day we seem to see you
Holding out your tattered shirt
That has the optimum wealth of your kind heart
Written in its worn threads.
Your blue sky has raised a canopy over the desert,
And the reach of your kind heart extends to the distant horizon.
I know not how that tempest of life blew
Into this barren landscape.
In just a flash clouds blanketed the sky;
The dark flag flies tortuously, struck down
By the invincible force of senility.
The dark, sere desert soil trembles in apprehension
On the horizon glows a leviathan Omar—
Lit by lightning-flashes.
In his shimmering glimmer wake countless earthen lamps.
In that sky and earth, so brightly lit up
Rides his Commander-in-Chief, fearless as always.
The far corners of the earth gape in amazement
In the white heat of that lamplight.
Where the sky stretches limitless
Where the sun rises pulsing with color and light
There rise you, in your golden moment.
You traverse the horizon at top speed
And cross deserts and mountains easily
Relaxed, without anxiety.
O Fearless One! Ever were you devoid of trepidation—
The lightning-brightened day gleams in your weapons

The fugitive who fearfully flees your sharp eyes
Us the Devil—yes, he himself, strong, invoking terror
Yet like a single discarded feather in front of the storm.
Facing the harsh reality he pales in paralyzing fear
And in a mere instant he flees the light
For the dark regions
Where the glow of truth is dimmed
By a wall of sins.
There your sharp saber rears like a crash of thunder.
In just one instant the wall breaks up
Into hundreds of bits and pieces
In the darkness the summit of Marble Hill
Suddenly looms large ahead
Bringing along a paragraph of the Great Truth
With an open palm cutting the demarcation line
Or even yet the sword flashes once more
At the head of the oppressor, the Sinner and the Tormentor.
The eyes are dimmed, the glance of the fog lights up!
In the unimaginable heart of that valor is the Great Truth
The golden eagle lit up by the rays of the Universal Prophet
Has spread her foamy bright wings the world over.
Bearing aloft the standard of the Invincible Peace
The victorious scimitar returns home at last.
O what manliness! On the capacious breast that peace lit up
There is a lot of pleasure. Faruque distinguishes
With alacrity between truth and falsehood.

And then again we see him weeping alone
At the head of the hungered masses
The night-watchman, who with eyes bleared
By sleep deprivation
Bears the burthen on back and shoulder.
That dimming flame of humanity alone in the desert
Has Omar, the Ruler of the Faithful, as a caring ally.
In his compassionate hands he holds the legacy
Of the Ultimate Prophet, to represent him.
He is the Representative of the Muslims, a devout Muslim himself
With a heart full of weal for the whole creation
With the layers of his compassionate being saturated with tears
He bears aloft the Standard of Grace for mankind.

*   *   *   *

The Great-hearted leviathan in whose hands
Rests the satiety of orphans
Who have no inkling at all that it was he, Faruque himself
Who cooked for them when they were hungry.
Sleepless are his long nights
In service to the poor, the destitute and the impoverished.
His servant seems to come to work
For those women who cannot help themselves.
When the earth burns hot
The lone Caliph goes seeking his camels
He is the ruler of the state treasury
The best helper and servant of all.
I know the impecunious is as dear to the Muslim world
As the destitute,

You have not the little money to buy a spoonful of honey
And so, you spend your days beyond counting
Sick in bed.
If the people see fit, they feed and pay you.
On the field of equality
You bear the standard of victory with the masses.
O Generous One! To you come the masses
With their petitions
Gladly you meet those demands
O Great Heart, Philanthropist!
The wayfarers find their way to you
Dearest relative, O Great Soul!
Your poor brother takes
Your torn shirt off your back.

You spend the lean days of famine
In near-starvation
You who dole out food at a hundred soup-kitchens
And infuse life into humanity.
Your sky is profoundly peaceful
The horizons echo with news of it
O Omar! In your liberal heart here
A million suns find sanctuary.
All the stars have recognized you as
The caravan-keeper of the silent night,
All of the homeless destitute
Have found in you a boon companion.
When humanity falls, you wake
Breaking the manacles of injustice,
And tearing with a hard kick

Through the ponytail of sin
That all oppressors sport.
You have struck at the heart of
All petty meanness.
In that whirling stream is a dream of the vast ocean.
Then let all meanness break apart
For truth and justice.
Let that lost day speak again to this night.
May the sword and the whip come to this hand of mine
To strike the final blow at this sullied life.
Where these shameless beasts devoid of humanity congregate
To obliterate the radiance of religion in the curtain of night
Lash Omar's whip to bring there the way to deliverance
Bring forth the brightness of freedom and break the apprehension
Of Mother Earth.
The Heroic Representative of the Great Prophet!
Let the day that he wanted
Be colored in beauty in our hands.

Today there is a crying need for followers of Omar
To walk forth in every direction
And carry burdens across fields with all their might.
You, the destitute, are seeking everywhere
Those who would make crops grow on the fallow fields
Of a barren night.
Those whose lightning whips strike the neck of oppressors
And whose kicks berate the bones of tormentors
Purer than fire, eager, flaming
With the coffers of their hearts overflowing with empathy
Those who have flung open the narrow bars of meanness

Lurking in the mind
The magnanimous heart is reflected
In the mirror of another generous heart
That ferocious yet pacific midday sun
Lights up the dream of an oppressed world
The object of daily meditation.
Then let that sunlight burn through this night
Obscured in darkness
O Leader of the Caravan! We smite the path
That first you trod.
Let these artificial lies and illusions burn up
O Caliph! As your whip lashes out from my hands
And as it wakes beholding the doors of the weary oppressed.
Let the small desire forget its dream
And all its garrulous talkativeness
As it immerses itself in activity
And takes upon itself your peaceful quietude.
The caravan that advances through the eloquent silence
Endlessly, day and night
Where the lance flashes in daylight in the driver's hands.

The hooves of the camels churn up the dust
As they run on intently seeking the fingers of the hero.
The tempest of the deep woods awakens
In the bell of warp speed,
Where the greathearted Omar has forgotten everything
Under the canopy of a desert sky.
His capacious breast fills with an enormous tranquility.
He knows the truth of the stars, the path of the sun
And yes, he knows where forests and hills

Fly as dust.

Ruler of the Faithful, the great hero who leads the caravan

Has led the big crowds by signals, day and night.

He is the Caliph of the Muslims, the Representative of the Faithful.

In his heart is the image of complete weal for all mankind.

Sword in hand, he holds the rosary too, the compassionate chief

He who has opened the myriads of rusted portals

On the way to the Ka'aba.

O Caretaker of the mosque at Madina! Greatest of all sweepers

You sweep away all the slime in the human soul.

O Friend! The law that is rock-firm

In your liberal hands

Makes the rich and poor equal.

In the rays of that justice, bright as sunlight,

There is no jot of injustice.

All are equal in those edicts

Laid down by the Prophet(Pbuh).

You have put an end to all inequity

And indeed all segregation,

Making the roses sing

In the heart gladdened by peace and equality.

Carrying the blooming flower of a great life before all

The flute of his caravan plays on in unstoppable love.

What strange hues color this still night

As the Darkness of petrification is torn apart

by the brightest of flames.

In the felicitations of a new direction
The fiery Borraq listens to the call of the date-arbors
In the Simoom of the Seven Saharas.
Among the myriad stars he glows
In radiant brightness.
The burning pain of Omar's memory is
In the foundations of creation.
The desert has died today
Rendering the Ship of the Desert immobile
The tide of night and day flows
In countless dust-storms.
The lament of death, raging thirst are here
In the hot wind.

The Night-Watchman Omar is not
Awake here anymore.
Even so, the breath of the past fills the world,
O Omar, Compassionate Friend,
Great-Hearted One!

OSMAN GHANI

Immersing in plumbless silence, O Welkin!
You have watched sleepless
Night and day, day and night merge into the dust
Like a caravan of camels
The endless temporal procession of numerous human beings
And the hues of the heavens—white, saffron, red and blue.
Only the coral worship minaret under the swift-moving tide of dust
Has raised its message of victory in a dream of green isles.
The man who achieved fullness in contemplation of coral
Is the only one whose memory lives in this dust,
That lightning truth is eternal;
Osman, Osman Ghani!
In the Arab world
And the blue skies of Madinah,

In the fields, woods and grasses of Ta'ayef
Down the spine of man
Along the form of woman
Raising a melody in profound darkness;
Much dirt has turned to dust
On the bodies of the populace
Only he who achieved his ultimate fulfillment
In the spiritual world
About whom the wayfarer of Madina speaks
To this day
That truth—the lightning bolt of denial
Osman, Osman Ghani!

He who placed his hand in the Prophet's(Pbuh) and got
Freedom from fear

He in whose shadows the wayfarer sat to find
A haven in life
Gentle and slow, emptying out his royal palace
That wayfarer filled his heart with the great savings.
Where the Basra Rose blooms, and the juicy pomegranate bursts.
The narcissus is bringing forth the shadow of the Gulmohor
Which is the flood tide of richesse, a portal to perfection
Where the royal pleasure-house has gone bankrupt over and over.
Where the peridot, the topaz and the turquoise crowd in
Over each other
The heart of the earth is replete with the weight
Of all these treasures.
Where the radiance of the light awakens the eternal amazement,
Putting the Kohinoor—yes, even that Kohinoor, I know, to naught.
Even yet the tree atop Mount Sinai—with her form of soil
Is spreading love on earth in emotion and relaxation.
Are you that tree on earth? Or the olive?
What a truly unquenchable flame of truth burns
In the heart of your love!
That love, pulsing pinkish red in the heart, came down
Saturated in color
Where the flame of the desert rose has merged into midday heat
In your own ruddiness! Have you opened the gold petals
In the skies over Madina?
The wealth that the layers of your innermost mind hoard
In the pinky-white moonshine

The saffron-hued complexion is diffusing

An unknown fragrance! See, it's all over the sky.

O Lovebird! The love song that you raised in the universe

Still holds in its thrall Arabia and Iran.

I remember, in the saddest night of nightmares on earth

You brought down to the Sahara Desert

The innermost truth of love . . .

The wings break off with strike upon strike

It chokes one, to cease all calls

Even yet you wander about, calling out

And they would smash that bud of truth to powder . . .

And yet you make flowers blossom, singing tunes of enlightenment

Raising an island above the endless bloody tears of a heavy lethargy.

This pain-smothered day still meditates

On the ancient tale of those days.

Behold the flag unfurled to the sky in high honor.

Whose royal pleasure-dome was liberated

By generous donations?

O Best of the Wealthy! 'Tis yours!

'Tis yours, Osman Ghani!

Scarring the sandy breast of Madina that donation of yours

Has brought a flow of life, distant-traveling wayfarers come

Dreaming of sure faith in a field of death.

On the day you establish that fact

Your huge coffers have recognized

The path to faith.

You gave endlessly

To eternalize the high honor of mankind

Upon this earth.

O Ever Courteous! O Ever Genteel! You spilt your own blood
So mankind could be free.
Lo, by your reverence even the Prophet's(Pbuh)mind is discomfited.
Even angels in heaven are humbled, seeing you
As they sing welcome to Osman, on either side of the road.
He who collected the Koran to keep the honor of truth
And gave up the shirt off his own back to keep the prestige
Of the shirt itself
That hero, of the true courage, meditates
On the truth
He, the sinless, coral-white, who knew not
How to attack meanly.
Ever-magnanimous, he believed firmly in mankind
And used his inner tranquility to mend
What had been rent asunder outside,
The scarred human spirit! He did not squander
The sacred charge left to him
By the Holy Prophet(Pbuh).
He is magnanimous, the Great One, giving his wealth away
Until he was destitute.
Even so, who complains about him today?
Who is the knowing sinner doubting his integrity?
What unbeliever calumnizes as a lie
The affection that engulfs everything and everyone,
Escaping its fetters from the mountain
And fertilizes one's desert heart?

Who is the faithless one that
Dares to speak ill of him whose generous donations
Have made this locality more beautiful

Who did not save even his last picayune lest he himself need it

Nor take even a morsel from the state granary?

His soul, expansive as the sky above,

Loved one and all equally.

In his open sky was an invitation to every star.

He loved all, yet did not show favoritism to his kin.

Upon his openness there was no concealment.

He whom neither power of state nor greed for money

Could ever entice,

Is the one now being accused of inappropriate nepotism

By liars.

Indomitable! Firm! Uselessly they blame him

For cowardice! He is a laborer, fighting

Ceaselessly for the truth to emerge victorious

In all directions, to all horizons

He has trampled the insolent animal pride down to dust

As if carelessly, the fearless warrior. Behold

The insolent vanity of Rome

Biting the dust. Behold, too,

The reaches of the state.

The deputy leader representing the Prophet(Pbuh)

Was the stalwart representative, as well,

Of all free people.

Even then his heart was immersed

In the deep sea of love.

He sought freedom, not the death of a brother

He could not take a life; instead, he sacrificed his own

For the weal of all.

He is not the one to disbelieve a faithful comrade

Yet on his chest are serpents sighing black venom.

When Marwan stabbed him secretly in the back

He, Servant of Religion

Was putting together the Holy Koran

And so building up the truth.

His killer chose his own secret way;

The sharp sword kissed his throat

And thus the Meditator on truth fell down the dark abyss

That is death's eternal slumber.

By the hunter's weapon the great bird

Went to his last home,

Leaving behind all the memories, spreading

From horizon to horizon,

And an enormous prestige.

Through the ages

So many passengers turned to dust in the Sea of Dust

(We are the dust mites, at our head

All consuming Time points the finger)

Only, in that tide of death, the island declares victory

Atop a coral minaret.

In the formations of Man, it is spoken of;

He has attained the ultimate fulfillment,

The brightly lit lightning brand of truth,

Osman, Osman Ghani!

ALI HAIDAR

His roar echoes from hill to hill, waking up the desert dells
Lo, Ali Haidar! Ali Haidar! There comes Ali Haidar!
The desert sun flies at his horse's hooves, and
The dream of the sun gleams in his scabbard.
What did flash out over the horizon yonder?
Was it lightning-fire, or Ali's sharp double-edged Zulfiqar?
The horizon has filled up, making it nigh impossible to see.
In the clash of the thunder wakes the chronicling of the fire-edicts.
Does the Tiger of Allah leap from the hillside
With his keen eyes trained on the enemy's throat . . .
With no time to spare Ali Haidar has broken the door down
Here comes Mortuza the Commander, breaking down the ramparts
Flee with your lives, mountain sheep, the sky is falling
Lo, Ali Haidar! Ali Haidar! There comes Ali Haidar!
The fields are a-tremble, the date-fronds are falling apart
As if the lightning has burnt through the canopy of date palms
Ali's Zulfiqar flashes intensely right and left
In the just-risen sun which heralds in the noontide.
Where indeed then is that sword
Which blinds the eye momentarily?
Where is Mortuza? Where is the girded one?
Here it is deep and dark.
Here the darkness seems ancient and unmoving
Like massed clouds
Carefree flows the sea of impediments in this place.

Here blows a dust-storm,
That scatters leaves;
I cannot lift up my feeble head
In this tempest.
Ali's Zulfiqar flashes not out like lightning here
And here for days the door to a desert lane has been rusted shut.
Even so I seem to hear a live roar in the immobile field
Even to this day the sword seems to sing in my veins
It is dearer than dear, I see drawn on the horizon
The Zulfiqar? Or curved lightning?
Images of a distant day . . .
Tearing apart the darkness of night from the world
Rises the Sun of Arabia
With the light-blinded Devils shooting arrows at his heart
And bringing to him a mountain of hindrances.
The young hero came to stand beside him just then
Sword in hand, devoid of fear
With a firm body carved seemingly of the stones of Mount Sinai
All its nooks and crannies alight with the illumination of the Hera
And the light of the Koran
It shakes itself out of all the torment
With liberal arms stanching the flow of the volcano
Half-insane, insensate in the zeal for Islam
He opens one by one the ever-closed prisons of humanity.
In his call comes the voice tearing through the open expanse
His call makes the heavens quiver
And the desert field crack up
Roars the Lion of God: Allah, Great is Allah indeed!

Ali Haidar, Soldier of Allah Almighty
Came to stand beside the Prophet(Pbuh).
Leaping down from the hill, the Tiger of Allah Almighty
Darts fiery sharp eyes at the throat of the foe.
I know not what Death Angel of tormentors
Makes even stone-hard hearts tremble in fear like a cotton boll.
How fast and furiously the storm blows across the desert!
Even this cold dead forest seems to have been lit on fire
Myriads of horses stamp on, raising millions of sparks
And the curved horizon flies before it.
The ground underfoot disappears as fast as arrows
With a tempest of death in the blood of martyrs
In the season of life.
With that, the double-edged sword glows at hand like a deadly cloud
Which is torn apart in a mere instant by the sun's rays
Like sharp weapons shining through.
The Zulfiqar starts in hand like a cloud
The cloud roars after tilling the field of the struggle,
'Ho, Ozza! Ho, Hobal!'
The locusts come shouting
As do the barbaric non-believers
The sea of slime spews foam
Filling the barren earth
With horribly mean ferocity
Scream the devilish impure ones
'Ho, Ozza! Ho, Hobal!'
He will tear the throat of Islam
And that of humanity
With his fierce mails of animosity
Draping surroundings in a dark curtain

He will extinguish the pure lamplight.
The infidels come screaming
Their shouts filling the atmosphere
'Ho, Ozza! Ho, Hobal!' . . . .
Where is the commander now? Listen to him call
'Lo, Ali Haidar! Ali Haidar! There comes Ali Haidar!'
Wherever he points his fearless finger
The skulls of infidels fly like stones
Azazil quakes in terror at the sound of that thunderous voice
And the black hearts of all the devils are broken asunder.
Tearing apart the cloud-cover of the spear and the mace
The sunlit sword paces the brinks of death
Winning over the enemy's lair rises the voice
Of that ever-victorious one, 'God is Great!'
O General, by your call the eternal Islam
Raises the victory-standard emblazoned
With the eye-pleasing white moon and star.
From the plumb-less depths rises the voice of a profound peace
And the sky twinkles with her myriad star-lamps.
O Great One! You do not wield just the sword
You have stabbed with truth the excesses of falsehood.
No blemish has ever sullied your pure mind
You never owned anyone but Allah as your Master
Whose edicts you obeyed, holding your head
Above all sinful servitude.
Those who serve not Allah, but are themselves
Caught up inescapably in the chain of slavery.
Rising far above these bootlickers of devils
He has left behind the path for great spirits to tread
The one whose spear has cultivated a million skulls

The dust from whose feet collected as a cloud over Badar
Lo! There he walks behind the Jew, his head lowered in reverence.
The humanity of the earth watches entranced the humility
Of this great soldier.
When conscience lets ye not push a senior citizen aside
Even the foe gets his due of human dignity from ye.
Your humility rode up to the Assembly of God Almighty Himself
So that no one can take away your right to assemble.
I know you wielded your sword only in the Path of God Almighty
Ever-abstentious, you never turned tormentor
You never took revenge, even when non-believers spat on your face
Servant of God Almighty, you suppressed all your wrongful anger.
Your humanity raised you above even the angels.
O Sufi Devotee! Just so, you have won over
The impassability of the sky.
O Great Portal of the Metropolis of Knowledge!
The illuminated knowledge of Tasawwof
That pervades the whole being
Raises the tune in a grove of rushes
By a quiet signal
Immersed in the ray of love, pain
Shimmers in the lamp-holder.
Millions of Muslims have reclaimed
The empire of their hearts.
I know not how the radiance of the seven heavens came
To the desert sands, a handful of dust, a fistful of earth.
From the depths of the sky he gleans the celestial notes
In the ribs of the earth his melodies of days long gone
Are played again.

He runs to the Reservoir of Kaosar, the Abode of Mahmuda
Where the flowering branch fills with dew,
And the Elixir of Eternity.
The nightingale flies up, the song of the rose in her heart
The hot desert wind whistles on the guava branches
Beholding the oasis on his path, the desert sun smiles
And the intense rays of the daylight hours sinks
Into a dreamy slumber.
The insane one who lost his way with the conflagration
Of the deepest hell burning in his heart
With the rush-flute you taught him to play
On his lips.
He has gone berserk in insane love
When the sea-eagle spreads out her wings
Over the desert.
You know the extent of her weariness
And the millions of dead forests twinkle in the smile
Of masses of flowers.
On the prayer-mat you pour out your nectar, O Devotee!
An unknown cup bearer pours out the wine of love
From Firdaus.
Your heart crosses the field like a blue pigeon
And even the arrows plucked off countless bodies
Does nothing to break her trance.
You borrowed speed from

The sun in whose rays you bathed yourself
Shunning diamonds and pearls
To expedite the progress of the human mind.

Humanity, irritated in the decaying garbage,

Achieves fullness by advancing the moon

Through her sixteen phases.

In the river of the moon the beams clamor

Ceaselessly

As on the pink palms of the desert damsel

The cymbals sing in sweet notes.

On the exterior of Mount Sinai

The thunderbolts form a ring

Even yet in its heart

Spurt and flow the fountains

Ali Haidar, here carved in stone! The life of Abu Torab

Flows as an endless fountain over impassable stones.

To what restless ocean is its turbulent speeding

Sprinkling bouquets of flowers on either bank

The desert river flows along

Diving with the best divers, she yet cannot

Find the sea-floor.

Ever newer flow-tides are pouring floods

Into the veins of the Tigris.

In plumb-less depths flows the limitless ocean water

At whose doors all frivolity ceases in reverence.

The endless hydraul plays in the sky like the tabor

The fiddle and the viola are blended as one

In the incantation of the player.

There isn't a moment to waste

Where the fiery passion of love transcends the layers of sky

There you roam daily, unhindered.

On the way to Jannatul Firdaus, the heart acknowledges
No loss at all.
O regal gateway to the metropolis! Your sky is open!
In front of you passes the sedan-chair of the fairy.
O Seeker of the Light! Who keeps tabs on that?
He has no time to, in quest of the Al Ahad.
He has submitted himself wholly to Allah the Almighty
So he does not care for the bonds of oppressors or tormentors.
So when Khyber the desert pass of the closed door calls
Your double-edged Zulfiqar flashes out in the sun.
Muslims never concede defeat
His victory is perpetual in all the world
O soldier, all these Khybers have closed their doors to ye
The sand-towers have collapsed as in a storm
His days were spent near stony trenches
When the tent of the Koresh has flown off in the tempest
Where the captive Bani Koraiza quakes in deathly terror
The timid King of Jandal flees, seeing the spear far ahead
And the days of the truce are past.

In the meantime, when the impassable road called,
The double-edged Zulfiqar flashed out in the sunlight.
I know that the Khyber has fallen to you exactly
As the lion's talons tear at the neck of the timid lamb.
At the edge of the darkness I see the new moon rising
Islam the religion has spread the world over
The poet is riding fast on the Arabian steed
Without time to stand and stare.

The great hero Haidar has broken down the closed door of the fort.
Following on his footsteps come Khalid,
And yes, Tariq and Musa too.
Floating down the port of the early morn
Comes the crimson dawn
There is no time to seek that road now
A new crier runs carrying the good tidings
Of victory.

The Prophet's edicts have spread
Like the rays of a victorious sun.
Colorful rose-petals are coming awake
In the foundation-stones of Iran.
The Great China listens intently for some lost footstep
The Abyssinian heart clamors under its black skin
Fearless, the oppressed climb the minarets
Of Madina today.
The seasonal flame pervades the soil
Of the limits of the bloody yet happy day.
The closed walls of eight forts have become dust today
So the crest of the new moon may be seen
From all the world over.
His call is heard, followed by the voices of the populace:
Lo, Ali Haidar! Ali Haidar! There comes Ali Haidar!

FOLLOWER OF LOVE
(ORIGINAL: PREM PANTHI)

He who has traveled the complicated path of love for a long while
Has seen the walls of impediment level out in his sight
Farhad's flame of love has brought his beloved to the light
He'd needed this thorn to hold the rose to his breast.
This separation, this pain of parting was very necessary . . . .
The souls of a myriad hurting lovers keep awake on this earth
As a fiery, passionate dream
Bearing the many slings and arrows of pain
That mark the way from the impassable realm of death
To the vibrant abode of life.
Myriads of igneous rocks, burning in the fire of separation
Would call him who would drink the cup
of the Oneness of God Almighty to the dregs
And saturate his loveless life in the wine of that Oneness
To test his devotion.
Knowledge could ne'er satiate that thirst for life.
The first word of creation is Love,
And only Love, naught else.

GHAUSUL AZAM

(ORIGINAL: GHAUSUL AZAM)

The Jilan sun beckons to an impassably rocky road . . . .
That full sun keeps on beckoning over and over
O, let the rays of the Jilan sun provide sight
To him who, leaving the caravan, gropes in the dark.
Let the new sunrise beckon out of a sky
from which the darkness has gone
Shedding bright light on this dark and moonless night.
Let the Jilan sun, like a strong lion, fearlessly
Shine down in searing hot rays.
O, bring the fierce life-fire of the Jilan sun
To this country of dark ways, conquered by the baser instincts.
After this dead, sullied night, pray awaken
The light of Truth; behold the unending path to fullness
Of all the skies and seas,
And the concealed mountain of fulfillment in every speck of dust.

KHWAJA NAKSHBAND
(ORIGINAL: KHWAJA NAKSHBAND)

O vigilant one, thou hast colored the earthen pitcher.

Maybe the earth speaks—the earth of the being speaks for certain.

The bird comes from a strange hill to build her nest

And fills it with song, flying off when it's time . . . .

Flies off, flies off. (The bird always keeps quiet

As does the earth) Your earth speaks out.

Your earth and wind, being in the life-fire of the sea,

Seeks the hour to set out; then, in time,

It leaves the flock of birds and soars heavenward

That is no earth. O Soul! To which difficult unknown region

Hast thou set off at last, having decorated the pitcher

To what destination, pulled inexorably by a lover?

O Conqueror of Death! Let my soul

Inundate itself in the attractive silent song of memory

And thine absolute Truth.

MUJADDID ALFESANI
(ORIGINAL: MUJADDID ALFESANI)

The new moon that had risen from shore to shore of the world

After millennia, piercing the Hindu temple

And striking down the numerous falsehoods

Of Nimrod's ranged idols

With a great blow, signifying the life-force of a million oceans

Bringing a flood of life to millions of dried up gardens

A free flow of life!—Then, it could not close the prison-door.

Selim's helmet was trampled in the dust

In the indomitable tide of truth

That the free-spirited Meditator had unleashed.

In that deep sea arise the waves of knowledge

(That had once radiated out of the stony roads of Sirhind)

Not pain, not suffering, not bitter sorrow

could rub out that life-force.

Not even the swords of the vain Moguls could stop it.

After a millennium that free sun lit up by the light

Of the Oneness of God Almighty

Brought forth the picture of Medina.

MY MIND

My mind is a whale in the approaching dusk
Submerging itself in the ocean of night,
Yet still I hear the sound
Trapped in the breast of the earth, coming from afar.
The sun has effaced his colors on the weary
minaret of the dusk clouds.
Even the wind has lost his velocity today
He does not understand before falling fast asleep
That there is no peace in the sea of darkness.
Even so, the dreams of a heated acceleration collect in the mind
In the languid motions of the wan, tired nerves.
Perhaps in the weary welkin of Chaitra
the inkling of a storm is moving
And millions of specters crowd in like a horrific nightmare
Fust then, thousands of thunderbolts clap in mine mind's sky.
I hear the celestial sound.
Your unfortunate night has brightened in
the free Eastern light of the dawn.
In your forest the ancient tree has shed its old sere bark.
The thought attacks like a fire on the horizon
Awakening in the minds of the weary throng
The sway of the hint of lightning-seared clouds in Baishakh.
Leaving the ocean of night, the mind becomes
A bird flying free in the sky.
Lost in the welkin, the wing leaves behind the old fallen minaret
And the myriad hues of the heavens, the horizon;
Like a prisoner's dream the mind is chainless—my mind.

51

PERIL OF DEATH
(ORIGINAL: MRITYU SANKAT)

Who the senile corporealist calls thee opium?
Who spreads the evil mantra of the Devil worldwide
Forgetting the identity of the soul midway to the brain?
Who has laid waste the peaceful field of the mind?
The primal soul of man wanders the road weeping.
Who is that barbarian who has immersed himself in devilish clamor?
What illusion has turned the blind Abraha to defend himself?
Will the darkness hide the sun? The storm blow
Dishonored, strangled? The doubt of this immobile night
Find itself a spot on the field as an unmoving, senile mass?
Will the vibrant river whose flowing waters
claimed the life of Pharaoh
And whose flow even Nimrod's stone walls could not curb
Forget her identity entirely?

SULTAN OF HIND
(ORIGINAL: SULTANUL HIND)

The night when the radiance of the new moon lit up the whole sky
Hiding Indraprostho under a deep blue curtain
That was the night when thou, O Meditating One,
Brought the hope of eternal life, keeping thy lover's heart
And fatigue far away.
Life-fiving, cleansing waters washed away
The poison of millennia
(The falsehood that had permeated the sullied soil of Hind).
The flow of the Waters of Life spread benediction on her heart.
The night wind shone bright by the light of the eternal Truth.
Thou brought'st the dream of a new life with the new sunrise
From then on, thou hast been
The one and only Sultan of Hind!
This unspent life has never beheld the flag of an emperor
Nor has the fire of any lover burnt so eternal.
Thou, and thou alone, hast conquered a million hearts
By a flood of love daily, and thus remain'st
The one and only emperor of a lover's heart.

TEARS DROP BY DROP

These rare teardrops of yours
Are as unfathomable as undimpled pearls.
On my dry sere body they raise the roar
Of a myriad of oceans full of holy Zamzam waters
I behold the Oceans Seven as in a dream.
In themselves your tears conceal the treasures
Of this vast solar system
Every dream, all the light and dark hide therein.
Those that thirst after your soul—
In the early afternoon glow they define people's tears
And throw open the portal to the blood-red dawn.
The message that whimpers in the Master's fiery Tartarus
That all but loses itself in the thirsty flow of lava
That seeks but fails to find itself
In the wide blue sky, earth or water
That reveals its brimming heart in endless, bitter pain
Flares up day and night in the incarcerated layers of the heart
That message, full and complete, emerges washed
By an undimpled tear.

THE CASCADE
(ORIGINAL: MUKTODHARA)

The lively rush of the wine
In whose rapid flow I left mine signature
Does never listen to nay, forgetting not the name of the sea,
The inebriety which yet failed to bar the path of Karani with rocks
In the firelight of the heart it has beheld
The animated, unstoppable face of the lover. It has seen
Its dear friend, whose shadow fell
In the tide of every moment.
Oblivious of emotion, the people watch in amazement that beauty.
Moses' fulfillment edges his road, the fathomless meditating form
Of Jesus. He looked ere he asked
Through Khizir's eyne, on whose path the Prophet Ibrahim
Lit the flame of the Oneness of God Almighty! All by his lone self
He brought to the full tide of faith
The unlimited supplies for the road——
Those supplies which even to this day
Numberless caravans bear as they plod along.

THE EXPLORER'S ENTREATY
(ORIGINAL: OVIJATRIKER PRARTHONA)

Intoxicate me with your strong, all-pervading wine

That burns the heart of the desert of Medina

That the world is agog to taste

That enlivens the whole of the Arab Azam.

Set me drunk on the free flow of that wine

Heated by the elixir of life;

Signal the tempest by its fiery-hot touch

And bring the burning of the desert to this my pleasurable world.

With thine fiery touch ignite my veins withal

My high speed does not heed hills, rivers or forests.

My rambunctious horse jumps into the river

In which shaded field more shall I spread thy radiance?

Which field or forest has not heard the roar of this sea

That lives radiantly in the rapid tide of Time.

THE INKLING
(ORIGINAL: ISHARA)

At the corner of the horizon comes
the clamorous storm from the west
The momentary rambunctiousness and murmur
of dead forests will now cease.
The neighing of the Arabian steed of him
Who is setting up home on the back of it,
Clamors through the skies as if to break it into splinters.
O Desert Bedouin, thou with the sun-lamp in thy hand
Hast brought the lighted taper with thee.
Will thine storm replace with new the old leaves that have fallen,
And the still crowd get the message to move forward?
Will their horizon be split by a lightning-strike
And the clash of the thunder startle a dead mind?
And then, stars disappear in the blue sky?
Even later, does the homeless one build a home for himself?
Thou hast brought the tidings of joyous sweetness.
Farhad breaks through towering impediments with his axe.
Thine axe rises and falls
Setting the hills aquiver
And a flood of pain makes the mind's sky tremble, too.
The Faerie Queene, fresh from her bathe,
awakens in the fountain of dew—
The red rose blooms on the edge of the tray of blue sky,
And the seven-hued peacock of the rainbow spreads his plumage.

O my beautiful sweetheart, lift thine veil now,

And remove the black scarf hiding thy face,

So that the clouds of the nightmare are banished from thine welkin

And it emerge all unafraid.

Let the young fifteen-night-old full moon

Shine forth in her saffron glory—

She is mine, that full moon.

She shoots inklings at mine heart.

The welkin well knows the inkling of the earth;

In the stormiest of nights

She brings in autumn's sheaves.

Behind the grapevine, behold,

The veil of the adolescent is up.

My blood clamors as if to kill me.

Thus, look, the moonbeam sends an inkling

In the arbor of the grapevine,

Boon companion of the desert night,

She croons an unfamiliar melody as an inkling.

Or maybe the young woman signals,

Awakening the flower of pain

Her signal is beheld

In the wandering of the soul lost in the desert.

What sentinel awakes in the corner of the sky?

Myriads of stars glimmer there

What awakens there? The moon, or just an inkling?

I know your signal, so I keep returning, over and over

Farhad knows Shireen's closed doors.

His strong axe cuts down hill after hill

Bringing rough rocks to the plains he makes flowers bloom on them

And hangs a Basra-bud ear-stud onto Shireen's lock of hair.

Is the dead garden spreading new leaves in thine mind?
And are red and yellow flowers blooming on thine branches?
The coral flower, breaking myriads of pomegranates,
Is the white coral appearing on that breast?
Lying down on the bow of the horizon
Is his radiance shining on the colorless star?
Did the sky-high memory of Suleiman's conquest of the world
Awaken a radiance of ardent desire in thine breast?
O my Shireen, please open, open the door
Break down into bits the dark walls of the Palace of Sleep.
Look this way where the sky sparkles with myriads of stars
See the speedy Arabian steed without reins in the sky—
That raises a clamorous neigh in the cusp of the storm,
With his intoxication deepest in the whirlpool of speed
That not even the crooked irony of impediment can break
It takes but just a moment for that Arabian steed
to disappear out of the country.
The Necropolis quakes at the step from his strong hoofs
And the dead field awakens in the storm of his extreme speed.
Is the mind's sky awakening with a rainbow drawn on it?
Is the white half-moon appearing on it, as well?
Is the colorful Gulmohor blooming there, by fire?
Even though the fearful, destructive storm blows outside
Indoors thine soul reserves its own speed
Even today she bears forth the Song of Solomon,
about his conquest of the world.
That bird flies along the storm, keeping up with it,
Fearless in the annihilating wind, she spreads her wing to
Soar upward.

In the lightning-seared forest she raises a clamorous cacophony

Which brings forth in the tranquil blue the white moonlight?

Is that bird, a Baishakh on wings, flying aloft?

And art thou hearing from her strangled voice

the call of the tempest?

She will awaken the sleeping flowers and leaves

of the night in this storm

And bring forth a flood of life from horizon to horizon.

Behold, she has brought a pebble from the path of Hera on her beak

On the hard stone has bloomed a rose

Behold, on her wing she has borne a great gift, unforeseen

Presenting an inkling of the distance floats the throne of Suleiman.

The wind, like a hypnotized snake, travels a stony path

To bear thy throne to the door to the abode of the stars

Thou hold'st in thy fist the flower-breath of the earth;

A firm resolution is in thine eyne and heart, and a great hope too.

Suleiman beckons with an inkling

While the Throne of Suleiman floats on air

See, the flag with the white moon beckons in the sky.

Deep under the barren soil flowers an endless dream

Sleepy as it is, it still continues to seek

The road is blocked by a stony wall, even then the flood-tide pulls,

Suleiman beckons with an inkling

While the Throne of Suleiman floats on air.

Even now the life in the harem is unending in the date-palm arbor

Yea, even now the reserved nectar of the

dried date exudes from its branch.

Are you going to be fearful now, in this storm?

See, the peacock has spread his plumage in the oasis.

O Messenger, art thou carrying the news to a barren field
With weary footfalls?
Do devils crowd thy path and hinder thee?
Does thy troubled night pass in a hundred sleepless darknesses?
Are the seven mirrors of thy mind fogged over today,
And the branch, sere and unfed, broken off at the frosty gate?
O Hero, thy battle armor is rusted over today
The land left fallow for so long has cracked up into smithereens.
Even then the stars twinkle and the moon shines an inkling in the sky
The dew drops like a fountain at the closed casement!
At the mouth of thy death-ocean is a taste of life
And in thine fasting endeavor of life
The Eid moon comes as a dream to be fulfilled.
Thine sere field, chapped dry and all cracked up
Beckons to the sky where massed clouds have begun to gather
Has that clamor sunk into the deep abyss of oblivion,
And has the stray star received signals from the moon?
Does the flame light the earthen lamp,
And is the dim veil of mist being torn through?
Has it responded? It comes, the fast wanderer,
Who has set up home on the back of the Arabian steed.

THE MARTYRS OF KARBALA
(ORIGINAL: SHAHID-E-KARBALA)

Lay down your burthen, O Rider, and behold

In front of thee the field of Karbala,

Where without a trace left of green, the endless sands

Burn like a fiery hell.

Whose lament engulfs the heaven and wind?

The wayfarer tree has foamy blood.

Today we stand on Karbala field, Hossain, alas!

We have dreamt of rivers of blood on Karbala field

Laments fill the whole world, and the sky too.

The world will be submerged, including peaceful Mecca Muajjamah,

Where if the oppressor wields his sword of torture,

he wouldn't be pardoned easily.

What infidel draws the dark curtain in the storm at day's end?

The invitation to Kufa fell through, so stand here alone,

To witness Yazid's sharp sword and listen to countless sighs of pain

See there in front the field of Karbala, like a curse!

Put down your load, O soldier, stand here like a fearless tiger

This life today has jumped to the throat at Yazid's hard torture.

The national flag's been shrouded in the black shroud of misrule

And the Royal Standard, a symbol of iniquity,

flies high in the blue sky.

The heart of the believer is burning

in the oppression of the infidel, oppressive sinner

As peace is slain in the blood of the humble peace-lover.

The flame of Hera flickers as the sun of Faran sets
Humanity covers her face and weeps in the court of bestial might.
Hark the footfalls of the enemy forces in the sere desert
The lance and the sword flash out, the clash rings in the far desert
Setting up base on the banks of the Euphrates,
the forces of Yazid parade
Set thine burthen down, Karbala has approached like death itself.
The timid and weak cling to life as they remember death
While the brave embrace death without fear.
However many the enemy are, issue the command, O Soldier,
We shall wake up the weary souls, jumping into the sea of death.
The desert field of Karbala shall be
the martyred soldier's final resting place
Issue the command today, O General, military leader.
Solemn thrill the war-drums, the enemy are
engaged, the fearful earth quakes
Respond, O Fighters for the way of Truth
Rend asunder the enemy formation,
On the banks of the Euphrates or in Paradise
The enemy march in battalions
Like a horizon-bow surrounding the earth.
Hark, Imam! Behold the amazed sun observing thy valor
Thine radiant manliness has dimmed even the enemies' gold crowns.
The weak and the timid cannot accept thine invitation to war
Making just a show of resistance, shooting arrows from far afar.
Thy chest parches with thirst, the thirsty baby wails at home
O Imam! Hear'st thou the women crying? Alas,
The Euphrates is closed off yet!
The Soldier of Truth has his final resting-place
on Karbala field at eventide

The Euphrates is closed off yet! There is
no news of its being conquered.
Though the sun hasn't set yet, the death mask of night descends
The sun of fortune is going down, taking
with it the life-force of the warrior,
The lament rises at the tent-door,
women and children groan in raging thirst,
The unknown night fills the skies with whimpers of deep pain.
O Hero! Having lost all thine companions, thou goest on alone
Like a lion wounded, bleeding profusely

O Conquering Tiger, what is this weariness
that engulfs thee as, by thine lone self
The day is ending blood-red as the sun sets on the Euphrates
The enemy shafts pierce thy heart, but thou
payest no attention, O Careless One!
The babe in arms has perished, for want of a mere drop of water.
Those cowards have shot a beautiful year-old baby to death
O Lion! Forget this weakness and awaken thine latent valor.
His chest pierced through, yet the lion has
conquered the bank of the Euphrates
He takes water from the Euphrates in his
cupped palms to wet his thirsty lips.
The water spilled from his palms as an arrow hit him again
And both banks of the Euphrates whimpered in terror.

The war-drums thrill in Yazid's camp, swords,
arrows and lances fly all over
The skies quake in fear, the dust colors with death
On that battlefield, the lone hero totters,
like a weary lion very near death
His wounded body falls like a large stone after being hit by the arrow.
He who gave his life to keep the honor
of the creed of his brave nation
Had his head severed from his body by his foe Shimar.
The setting sun covers his face his face in deep pain
The light of Islam goes out, struck by Yazid to utter darkness,
A heart-rending cry rises from Karbala field in spurts of blood
A lament fills the earth and sky; weeps
humanity: Hossain, O Hossain, alas!

THIS STRUGGLE TODAY

This struggle today is with yourself.

Today, to conquer yourself, you must march out bravely.

Deck all the horizons of your mind out in battle fatigues

In the temporal sky as well as in the mind's sky clashes the thunder

We have returned now to the greater endeavor

O Commander! Express all your chivalry now.

On the soil of your mind play the war-drums, bugles and clarions.

A victory this time around will open for you

the royal doors of the horizon.

The petty picture of envy lies in wait from base to base

Obstacles as high as mountains bring to

the fore the resolute hill of pride

Avaricious wishes, mean desire

The lolling tongue of the brazen, lowly comfort

The putrid state of the dirty insects in the garbage dump

And the exquisitely jealous bestiality of fierce animals.

The very grimed wolves lie in wait.

O Commander! Wield your great power here,

And march, march out in force

In the temporal sky as well as in the mind's sky clashes the thunder.

*

Today's endeavor is to know oneself

To buy and sell of humanity

In the crowded marketplace.

The time is now to pay all debts and square everything up.
Today is the right time to reimburse all that you owe—
The struggle today is with yourself to know yourself inside out.

*

The spume of death spurts from the mouths of this throng
Resentful of all this rottenness
The raven spreads his wings overhead
As his farewell call breaks over the shores of death.
Fierce Baishakh has come over the uneven stony ground.
Behold the great body of people, a portrait
of weakness and immobility—
Their sun has set at midday.
See their forests dim before their time.
For nothing have they sold themselves to the devil,
And having kissed his feet, stood in silence.

*

The heart wants to respond to this huge body of people
And sniff the scarlet petals of the narcissus
His heart trembles, though it is feeble in the clutches of death
Even now, his eyes look up eagerly towards the new horizon
As the eagerness for a new day pulses in his veins.
Today, the day is to awake and be awakened
Where Death has raised his lance
The last gift is to strengthen oneself.

With this new introduction to itself the tree has grown stronger.
The Si-bird has begun a new melody on its branches
The big tree wakes, having conquered her inner struggles
She has got the lively speed to raise her head high to the sky
Her branches shine colorful with fruit!
The struggle today is with herself to know herself inside out.

*

The victorious tree will stand out in this stormy struggle
Today the velocity is in the impassable
And not in the emotional outbursts of a drunkard.
Seek the horizon today in the sharp scrutiny of the sun
And do not ransack the seas and forests
In a blind person's paroxysm of emotion.
Form a new spirit and mindset
In a sleeping old body
And sow the seeds of a bright new morn
In the sere desert of the night.

*

In the fullness of each petal let the free flower of fire awaken
And let Mount Sinai stand at the very spot where the stones meet.
Let the Torah flow down there, and also the Glorious Al Koran
New floods submerge as the full contingent of believers gathers,

And yet again let an ever-new freedom come
as the Sun of Hera shines down
Let the Fighters for Justice inaugurate a new world.
Let them forget their slip of foot
Let them pick up the slipped foot
On the way the Devil entices in a million methods
And there are black dangers of the night
Crushing the mountain of obstacles underfoot
Today, we shall consolidate the mind.
Let the librated multitude seek the consolidated mind
In the individual.
That sun of humanity
Spends its nights under the distant veil of darkness
The power of winning himself
Awakens his horizons once more.
So the struggle is with oneself, today is the time to know oneself
Hark! In the temporal as well as the spiritual welkin
The thunder claps in unison.

THIS TUSSLE

This conflict that goes on endlessly
Enveloping the entire mind
Is on the shores of day and night.
The wolves bare their fangs every moment
Inflicting the venomous suffering that spells defeat,
He is poisoning the night
By the path to crooked meanness.
The dream is mine day . . . .
How far off indeed is that Kohinoor of humanity today?
In the sorrowing sky mine vanquished melody
Is concealed in the dark dungeon . . . .
All the beasts of the mind today
Have drunk so much that they are besotted—
My midday sky is heavy with sleep,
Drowsy and lifeless.
War-weary, it observes the complete bestiality
While its ultimate failure bangs its head.
The dream is mine day . . . .
Even so, it still raises the lance on the edge of night.

*

The pink petaled day blooms bit by bit
In a continuous cycle
The cannibals attack its every petal in hordes
Even so, every moment in bloom marches towards victory

Like the very first love
Filling the skies of the foothills with fragrance.
For just a while the leisure of a free day
And at least a moment to make the flowers bloom
Is all that I ask.
Let this war of night and day, this fear of defeat
This policy of retreat
Cease for just an instant . . .
And the sunlight of humanity bathe everything
In searing radiance . . .
All I ask is at least a moment
So that the deep blood-red petals may bloom out.
The worms of pestilence have set up home
In the chambers of this bug-infested, dead soul
Where now is the horizon of man? Far afar and yet farther on
The terrible tune of defeat sounds.
Bestiality flows in his veins today
The universal mind roams destitute.
He tries to raise his head even though
He is weak under the cover of endless darkness
The dream day is far off yet
The shaking of the pink branches of a dew-lapped colored blossom
The stars sparkle all over an unknown sky
. . . . An unhindered dream . . . .
So among the wolves rages its endless war.
Even as the cry of the earth
Sounds from sky to sky
This searing poisonous pain in mine veins
Pulls me inexorably lower and lower,

Yet all the covers are torn asunder in a cry for liberty;

Even so he is absent-minded under cover of intoxication.

Between the cloud-covers of this sky

The stars did beckon

And at the call of some impassable Mount Sinai

The prison became intolerable.

It was detestable defeat in the hands of the intolerant beasts.

On the impassable rocks yet waves the constant

half-moon standard of man.

Those who had first climbed the stairs of the mountain path

Still set this desert shore a-tremble with their momentum.

All the noise of the evil spirits stops

And the gurgling of that nonstop velocity

Can be heard far afar.

They've moved on, pushing aside all obstacles, crushing the beasts

To the rocky Mount Sinai . . . .

The sky of the sick mind spreads here a wind of death

The burthen of the distant mountain-climbers has waxed yet heavier

Even then they seek men among the wolves

And strike their swords on the head of bestiality.

Even if the wolf bares his poisoned fangs

Even if the pain of lowliness here is intolerable

Yet even so the distant summit of Hera has called

O friends, open wide the doors of your dwellings.

Point your sharp arrow to the forehead of bestiality

In this strife, this greater scuffle . . .

All I ask is at least a moment

So that the deep blood-red petals may bloom out.